Squeezing the Orange

Simple ways to live a full life

Jason Butler

WRITE BUSINESS RESULTS

This book was produced in collaboration with Write
Business Results Ltd. www.writebusinessresults.com
info@writebusinessresults.com

ISBN-13:978-1974663194

ISBN-10:1974663191

First published in the United Kingdom in 2017 via CreateSpace

Published by J & J Butler Consultants (UK) Limited, 44 The Pantiles,
Tunbridge Wells TN2 5TN
©2017 Jason Butler

For further information please visit www.jason-butler.com

"A cracking good read. The life advice in this book should pay for itself many times over."

Justin Urquhart-Stewart - Broadcaster and co-founder Seven Investment Management

"A really enjoyable, easy-to-read book with important life lessons for everyone. Bravo, Jason!"

Neil Darke - CEO The Life House

"Easy to read and packed with inspiring stories, this invigorating book will encourage you to live life to the full."

Dr Lien Luu - Associate Head of School: Enterprise & Commercial, Coventry Business School

"Jason Butler is a great communicator and I loved this book. He explores some exciting, simple, and important ideas that are relevant to anyone looking to live life to the full."

Brett Davidson Founder, FP Advance

"This is a great little book of wisdom that should be one of your life-long companions. Keep it in a convenient place and pick it up often, whenever you need inspiration or motivation. Jason reminds us that life is not a rehearsal, each of us only have a short time on this beautiful planet, and we have to squeeze the most out of life."

Paul Armson – Entrepreneur and author

"One day all books will be written like this! Short, packing a punch, and crammed with high value, actionable content that will (if used) make us all more effective. I loved the stuff on achieving big and taking responsibility. Life lessons for everyone!"

David Hyner   Professional goal setting researcher and motivational speaker

"Storytelling has been a crucial skill throughout history but like any skill it has to evolve to appeal to the next generation. 'Squeezing the orange' evolves in this way, providing humour, inspiration and strategies to take your life to a higher level"

David Hulman, Self-Belief Chief

"This book is right up my street and probably up the street of every driven, ambitious person on the planet! A great little reminder that it's not the big things that make us happy, but the little things every time!"

Michelle Hoskins Founder and Director Standards International

"Jason Butler has a wonderful style of writing that makes you smile as you learn. He has immense expertise, and delivers it in such an easy way that everyone will love it and benefit from it. Buy copies for everyone in your family!"

Alan Stevens Past President, Global Speakers Federation

"Jason Butler shares meaningful advice that will help you create a bigger, brighter future and he does it in a way that makes it all seem very possible."

Julie Littlechild Speaker, writer, and Founder AbsoluteEngagement. com.

"This is the only book you need to step into a better version of yourself. It is easy to dip into a chapter, each with practical advice based on real life examples."

Diana Malone - Yoga Teacher, Reiki Master, Thought Field Therapy

Acknowledgements

A big thank you to Georgia Kirke and her team at Write Business Results for their sterling efforts in helping me pull this book together. Georgia's enthusiasm and support has made the book creation process a very pleasurable experience.

Thanks also to Amy Highland for all her help with digital communications design and project management - you are an absolute star.

Thanks also go to all those friends who took the time to read the manuscript and gave useful feedback and words of encouragement. I am grateful to know so many lovely people.

Finally, a big thank you to my family for putting up with me. They remind me each day how great it is to be beautifully and wonderfully imperfect and different.

To my mother for constantly telling me that I could be anything I wanted to be in life.

Contents

Foreword

I had the pleasure of first meeting Jason nearly 10 years ago. Our initial meeting was prompted by Jason's desire to explore how he could enhance his personal and professional development journey, which was focused on optimising every aspect of himself and his life. A decade on, I now know that Jason's desire to continually improve and live his own life to the full, is unremitting and unwavering.

As a Chartered Psychologist, I specialise in coaching individuals and businesses to optimise their performance and become the very best that they can possibly be. I meet people every day who are ready to take ownership and make a change in their life so that they can break out of the 'tyranny of averageness' (see Chapter 3). The first step always takes courage and the process that then follows requires energy, effort and commitment. Jason is exceptional in his attitude and dedication to self-optimisation and the work he is prepared to put in to achieve it. Which is why, if you are ready to make a change in your life, I think you will benefit from reading this valuable and impactful book.

One of Jason's top qualities, in my opinion, is his generosity. He is very driven and committed to being the best version of himself and this is demonstrated in a variety of ways, throughout this book. However, Jason's drive is not a purely selfish pursuit. On the contrary, ever since I have known Jason he has been passionate about helping other people to thrive and optimise in whatever way possible. He does this by developing people that work with him as well as friends and family members, he seeks out opportunities for them, he connects people with each other, he openly shares his ideas and gives his time to others. This generosity has resulted in this book. Jason has managed to crystallise his lifelong learning and experience, concisely, into this book so that he can help a wider pool of people than would be possible in person. By sharing his valuable insights in this book, he can help you to live the full and rewarding life that you desire and deserve.

Reading this book may be your first step or one of many steps that you have already taken in your quest to make a change. In my experience, the first step is the most important one. Once you have made the psychological shift to do something differently, you are 'open' to ways of achieving this and are more likely to commit to a plan of action.

This book will help you not just to 'believe you can' achieve whatever it is that you want to achieve, it will give you ways of thinking about how to approach your goals in a meaningful and purposeful manner. It encourages you to look inside of yourself, confront your fears and challenge you to dare to aim higher and think big. It will empower, energise and motivate you. It will also help you to take an inventory of your life, your goals, your desires, your friends and support network and assess what you need to help you on your journey – which is critical if you genuinely want to make a change in your life. As Jason explains in Chapter 5 – if you want to make a change, then you need to change and step out of your comfort zone. This can be scary but it will also be liberating and you don't need to do it alone.

Many of us have books that we start to read, with great intentions, but only get through a few chapters, or even pages. This isn't necessarily because the book isn't useful, interesting or well written but more often it's due to the length of the book and the repetitive nature of the message or theme being communicated. This book is different in that each chapter is a stand-alone theme which can all help you to simply achieve a fuller life. It is short, concise and easy to read – quickly. The style is well suited to the way we tend to like to consume much of our content these days – bitesize.   Consequently, this will be a book that you can read and finish! It will also be a useful book to return to time and time again to help you stay on track toward your goals.

When Jason invited me to consider writing a foreword for this book, I jumped at the chance. Why? After all, there are a plethora of 'self-help' and 'motivational' books out there, some good and some not so good. What makes this book different and why would I choose to endorse it and encourage my clients and others to read it?

Because I trust and respect Jason – he has integrity, he is honest and authentic. Most of all, he is a living example of someone who practises all that he has written about in this book and he is living a full and rewarding life. He has generously shared his wealth of knowledge, experience and insight in this book, which I believe, will be incredibly valuable to anyone who reads it. So, if you are ready to make a change in your life, seize the day and read this book. Perhaps more importantly, I urge you to take it one step further and put into practice the many excellent ideas, tips and actions you will find in it. You will be grateful that you did.

Finally, I hope that the investment you make in reading this book and any related activities that you carry out, will give you bountiful returns by giving you what you need to live your life to the full and achieve your 'hairy and scary' dreams (see Chapter 28).

I wish you happy reading and an amazing journey of change in your life that you and your loved ones will all benefit from.

Dr Jo Perkins, C.Psychol. London, 2017.

Introduction

If you're reading this book then like me, for the last few years, you've been thinking about making a change in your life.

A change for the better; to achieve greater success and satisfaction.

This book will help you sidestep the time-consuming trial and error of finding ways to live your life to the fullest, and cut to the part where you see a positive impact on your happiness and wellbeing.

I was a financial adviser for 25 years.

Over the course of my career I interviewed nearly a thousand people.

I listened to their life stories; their successes, their failures, their relationships, their aspirations, their hopes and their fears.

I learned that it's not where you come from that matters, but where you are going.

I learned that the richest people didn't always have the most money, but a desire and ability to enjoy their life to the fullest, and not always for personal pleasure or benefit.

I learned that failures are a prerequisite to achieving any type of success.

I learned that putting things in perspective, being grateful for what you do have, and showing humility are all essential elements for a fulfilling life.

Above all, I learned that we all have different ideas of what it means to live a 'good' life.

But I also learned that few people have really taken the time to think exactly what a good life really looks like to them.

As the old saying goes if you don't know where you are going, you'll probably end up somewhere else!

Ricky Gervais, the British actor, musician and comedian made the following comment on Twitter a while back: "You're born and then you die, but that bit in the middle is f*****g brilliant."

Gervais's Tweet pretty much sums up what this book is all about.

I want your and my 'bit in the middle' to be brilliant.

I want you to get the most out of life, so that when you take your last breath you can say to yourself "I'm glad I did," and not "I wish I had" or "I wish I hadn't."

What follows is a collection of ideas, concepts, principles and insights which I've learned from my own life, that of the hundreds of people I have met through my career, and from the hundreds of personal development, self-improvement, business and biographical books I've read over the past 30 years.

Keep the book with you and dip in to read a chapter or two whenever you feel you need a boost, some motivation or encouragement.

Some of the ideas within these pages might seem obvious and perhaps already known to you, but that doesn't mean you couldn't benefit from a reminder - I know I frequently do - it's possible you're not actually putting them all into practice on a habitual basis.

The title of this book came from some advice I gave my eldest daughter when she was nine years old.

I explained that life is very much like squeezing an orange in that we have a choice over how much juice we squeeze out of an orange, and we have a choice over how much we get out of our lives.

Life really is what we make of it, and when it comes to meaning, happiness and satisfaction, I want you to really squeeze your own orange to get out of it every last drop.

The North Star

The key to getting and staying excited and motivated

"Change will not come if we wait for some other person or some other time. We are the ones we've been waiting for. We are the change that we seek."

Barack Obama, former President of the United States

In 1965 things didn't look good for Singapore.

This small island in Southeast Asia had just been expelled from a short-lived political union with its much larger neighbour Malaysia.

Unemployment was high, there was a chronic housing shortage, sanitation and healthcare were in disarray, and there was tension and conflict among its mainly immigrant population.

The majority view outside of Singapore was that it was a complete mess, and the prospects for survival were bleak.

Against this unpromising backdrop, Lee Kuan Yew became Singapore's first prime minister.

Lee immediately set out his bold vision for Singapore to move from being a third-world country to a first-world country in just one generation.

9

Despite all the problems the country faced, this ambitious vision gave the government and its civil servants a sense of purpose and long-term perspective that underpinned every decision and action that they took.

The government oversaw the building of a huge number of high-quality affordable homes, and a massive investment in education.

They invested in modern infrastructure and established state-of-the-art manufacturing sites that attracted investment from many large multi-nationals.

The government made English the common language to create cohesion and employability among the diverse population, but also allowed the population to learn their native language to preserve their cultural identity.

Above all Lee extolled the virtues of, and enshrined in law, the principles of multiculturalism and meritocracy.

The results have been nothing short of incredible.

Singapore is ranked 1st in the world for ease of doing business.

It ranks 1st in the Programme for International Student Assessment (PISA)*[1] rankings for educational achievement in science, maths and reading.

It is the 3rd most competitive country in the world.

---

[1] PISA is run by the Organisation for Economic Co-operation and Development (OECD).

It is ranked 3rd in the world for gross domestic product.[2]

It is ranked 14th out of 200 countries for low unemployment.

It is 2nd in the world for the lowest level of infant mortality.

Developing a bold vision or master plan is essential in life, in business, and in politics.

A big vision is the guiding light which galvanises you to take action, make difficult decisions, and to stay motivated in the face of challenges, setbacks and adversity.

Singapore might never have become the incredibly successful country it is today without Lee's ambitious vision.

So if you want to achieve amazing things in your life or your business, you need to have a compelling big vision.

It worked for Singapore, and it can work for you.

---

2 This represents the value of all the goods and services produced in each country, adjusted by the cost of living.

Kakonomics

How culture affects outcomes

Over a decade ago, two Italians - Gloria Origgi, a researcher and philosopher at the Jean Nicod Institute in Paris, and Diego Gambetta, a professor of sociology at Oxford University - began a conversation about Italian academic conferences, and how they didn't measure up to similar events they'd attended in Britain and France.

They decided to look into this situation to find out why.

In the introduction to their subsequent research paper Gambetta and Origgi gave the following context:

"Sometimes what goes wrong is timing, things do not happen when they are supposed to happen. Or they happen in a different form from that which was planned or are simply cancelled. Workshops have twice or half as many people as one was told to expect, the time allocated to speak is halved or doubled, proofs are not properly revised or mixed up, people do not show up at meetings or show up unannounced, messages get lost, reimbursements are delayed, decreased or forgotten altogether. This experience now extends to internet dealings: relative to those in other countries, Italians' websites are scruffier, often do not work properly, remain incomplete or are not updated, messages bounce back, email addresses change with dramatic frequency, and files are virus-ridden."[3]

They discovered that sometimes two parties involved in a transaction will have an implicit acceptance, and even expectation, of a poor outcome.

There is a cultural acceptance that being mediocre is the norm, and in fact anyone who delivers high quality is actually the odd one, because no one expects it.

This phenomenon of exchanges of goods or services, in which people prefer to give a low quality good or service in exchange for another low quality good or service, is known as 'kakonomics', from the ancient Greek 'kakos', meaning 'bad'. It literally means 'the economics of the worst'.

The phenomenon is also believed to be anchored in what is known as the 'perceived tyranny of excellence'.

Basically, people find the pressure of pursuing excellence to be too great, and find that having a chance to ease up a bit is appealing, so everyone accepts that 'mediocre' is okay.

[3] Origgi, G, and Diego Gambetta. 2009. "L-Worlds: The Curious Preference for Low Quality and Its Norms" Oxford Series of Working Papers in Linguistics

This thought process means you've failed before you've begun, because you adapt your mindset and behaviour to the prevailing - mediocre - culture that surrounds you.

You can see it in some groups of people, in particular.

When I was at school it wasn't cool to be bright.

And that was as much about the people around me and the way they perceived their own inadequacies, benchmarking themselves against others.

"THE FOLKS HERE CLAIM THAT YOU HAVE BEEN TRYING TO EXCEL"

But at 11 or 12 years old I didn't realise this, so I didn't speak too much, and didn't risk letting others think I was some kind of swot, because that was the way to survive.

It was one way of dealing with the situation, but it perhaps wasn't the most beneficial option open to me.

If we're around people who feel inadequate about themselves and are scared to try to be their best, they drain our positivity.

We might modify our excellence and hide our light under a bushel, because we're worried about outshining somebody and offending them, when really we should have the principles and self-confidence to do the right thing and aim for our personal best, whatever that may be.

I should have done that, but I didn't.

However, I thankfully did manage to find that mindset later in life.

There are two effective ways to avoid being subsumed into a culture of kakonomics.

You remove yourself from the environment - if that's possible.

Or you rise above it and set your own high standards and expectations, making others aware of the negative consequences if they don't do what they promise.

Above all aim to do your best every day.

Bland it Up

The tyranny of averageness

Some years ago I went for a meal at a nice restaurant with two of my friends.

After the second course of a seven-course tasting menu, I nipped to the bathroom, leaving my friends deep in conversation.

By the time I came back, my cutlery for the remaining five courses had been moved around.

As I eat left-handed, this was actually a very thoughtful thing for someone to do.

I asked my friends who'd moved my cutlery around and they advised that they hadn't noticed anyone.

It transpired that one of the waiting staff had noticed that I eat differently from the way the table had been laid out (conventionally, for right-handed people).

So they waited until I left the table, then came over - not even noticed by two chums who are at the same table - moved all the cutlery and glasses around, said nothing, and retreated.

Now that's above average service, isn't it?

The sad fact is it is the exception, not the norm, for people to rise above being average at most things in their life.

Would you like to be described as an 'average' lover?

Or of 'average' intelligence, looks, or income?

Or an 'average' driver?

"YOUR AVERAGE SALARY THIS MONTH IS YOUR AWARD, GOOD JOB!"

I doubt many people would put their hand up to claim averageness at any of these things, but there are plenty of things that so many people appear to be fine with being average at - because they've decided to settle.

I think sometimes people settle for average because they're frightened of trying harder and failing.

To be above average involves risking failure, and people often avoid making any effort to improve their lot in life for this reason.

Seth Godin put it like this in his great book The Dip: "Average feels safe, but it's not. It's invisible. It's the last choice - the path of least resistance. The temptation to be average is just another kind of quitting... the kind to be avoided. You deserve better than average."

Holiday on Mars

If you think you can...

"Whether you believe you can do a thing or not, you are right."

Henry Ford, founder of the Ford Motor Company

In September 2016, 45-year-old Elon Musk walked onto the stage at the 67th annual International Astronautical Congress in Guadalajara, Mexico.

He outlined two options: humans stay on Earth until we eventually become extinct, or they become a multi-planet species.

Unsurprisingly, Musk explained that becoming an interplanetary species is the favoured choice.

He outlined the various options for colonising another planet.

After discounting colonising the moon due to lack of size, resources and daylight, Musk explained that Mars was the best choice for the first human interplanetary colony.

"What I really want to try to achieve here is to make Mars seem possible - like it's something we can achieve in our lifetimes," he said.

Musk explained what needed to happen in order to enable humans to travel to and colonise Mars.

Like an excited physics teacher, he walked through the science, explaining the spaceship configuration, fuel type, flight sequence, as well as the challenges of landing and refueling on Mars, and creating a viable atmosphere.

Musk foresees a colonial fleet of about 1,000 ships, each holding 100 people, to eventually take 1 million people to Mars over 40-100 years.

He wants to get the programme started by 2025, and achieve inter-planetary human life in his lifetime.

Musk is worth well over $13 billion but he made it clear he isn't interested in money for his own use, "The reason I am personally accruing assets is to fund this. I really have no other purpose than to make life interplanetary."

Believing that you are capable of doing something has been shown to be a major determinant of success.

Psychologist Albert Bandura introduced the term 'self-efficacy' to describe the psychological phenomenon that enhances goal achievement.[4]

It is, he says, "The belief in one's capabilities to organize and execute the courses of action required to manage prospective situations."

In other words, if you believe you can do something you are much more likely to achieve it, and if you don't believe you can achieve it you are more likely to fail.

---

[4] Albert Bandura, Self-Efficacy in Changing Societies (Cambridge University Press, 1995)

This means that as well as setting life goals that are important and meaningful to you, you also need to believe that they are achievable.

People who have high self-efficacy also develop higher emotional resilience – the ability to bounce back from failure, mistakes or set-backs.

"BEST SELLER: 3 SECRETS TO SUCCESS"

They also see failure as a learning opportunity and use their past experiences to achieve success.

Along with Elon Musk, other examples of high-achievers with high self-efficacy (because they experienced significant failure on their route to achieving significant success) include Thomas Jefferson, Walt Disney and J.K. Rowling.

To increase the chance of your goals becoming a reality you can:

1. Break your goal down into a series of smaller, more achievable milestones, and celebrate the success of reaching them.

2. Find a mentor, friend or colleague to give you encouragement and support.

3. Paint a detailed picture in your mind of how your life will be when you have achieved your various goals, and what they will mean to you.

4. Cultivate happiness by integrating as many things as you can into your life which lift your mood and help you to remain positive - such as music, exercise, comedy, hobbies or social interactions.

5. Be pragmatic when you start to doubt yourself - accept you are only human and not perfect, but don't let it dominate your thinking.

6. Focus on progress towards your goal, not achieving perfection.

You might want to review your goals to make sure that they are still important to you and then recommit to achieving them.

Whenever you think you are starting to doubt yourself I suggest you listen to Journey's classic song 'Don't Stop Believin'.

Just make sure that you have it really loud!

Those old slippers

The secret to lifelong growth

> "Insanity: doing the same thing over and over again and expecting different results."
>
> Albert Einstein, theoretical physicist

Lucy Kellaway read Philosophy, Politics and Economics at Oxford University in the late 1970s.

After winning the Wincott Young Financial Journalist Award in 1984 she became a journalist for The Financial Times in London, where she wrote about topical management issues in a whimsical, tongue-in-cheek style.

Over the years Lucy published several books on management, won two prestigious journalism awards, and was in demand as a public speaker.

In November 2016, at the age of 57, Lucy announced in her Financial Times column that, as she wasn't getting any better at her work and wasn't enjoying it any more, she would rather take a chance and retrain as a maths teacher.

She went on to explain that from Summer 2017 she would work as a teacher in a 'challenging' London secondary school, although she would still write 12 articles a year for the Financial Times.

Lucy is a great example of someone who has stepped out of her comfort zone and taken a risk.

After 31 years as a full-time journalist and at the top of her game, working for a highly respected news organisation, she had decided that remaining in a job where she felt like she was standing still was just as much failing as trying something new and not getting on with it.

And she's certainly got a point...

No one ever grows inside their comfort zone.

People, relationships, and businesses never grow in their comfort zones.

You may keep your comfiest pair of slippers, because they're what you know and love, but eventually they fall apart.

If you want to change something, then you have to change something.

All or nothing

A simple approach for doing great things

Over the years I've heard various people mention the importance of having a 'work/life balance'.

The suggestion seems to be that we can't be happy, fulfilled or have meaningful xpersonal relationships unless our life is in 'balance'.

By 'balance' they mean that no one part of our life should dominate, or take a disproportionate amount of our time, attention and energy.

I've come to the conclusion that the idea of living one's life in balance is total tosh.

Whenever I've sought to achieve something in my life that wasn't easy, I've had to live my life out of balance, precisely because I needed to put all my focus, effort and time into that task.

For example, whenever I write a book I have a very busy few months getting the basic drafting done, which means I have to get up early, work late and say no to almost everything else.

When I've been preparing for a long distance running race or triathlon I've had to increase my aerobic training, eat a lot more and go to bed earlier.

When I became a professional speaker, I had to spend most of my time creating talks, learning them and continually practising my performance.

When I recently renovated a run-down house, I spent most of my days planning and coordinating the works, attending the site to liaise with contractors, and getting hands-on laying floors, hanging doors, painting and cleaning.

"I THINK DAVID'S DOG IS TAKING
THE GUARD DOG JOB TOO SERIOUSLY"

The point is that you have to go out of balance to achieve great things, particularly if they are new or outside of your comfort zone.

A round-heeled Woman

It's never too late to change your life

Depending on your literary tastes, you may not have heard of Jane Juska[5] - but once you've heard her story, you'll be unlikely to forget her.

Just before the Millennium, the retired high school English teacher was feeling that her life lacked drama.

She decided to change her life significantly, inspired by a French art house film she had watched, where a woman's friend places a personal ad on her behalf, so she might meet a new man.

On her way home from the cinema, Jane was musing on the fact that she'd had very little sex over the past 30 years, as well as considering how unfortunate it was that she'd never achieved her goal of becoming a published author.

So she chose to do something about both those disappointments, simultaneously.

---

[5] Read more about Jane's book at http://www.aroundheeledwoman.com

Jane placed a personal ad in the New York Review of Books:

"Before I turn 67 - next March - I would like to have a lot of sex with a man I like. If you want to talk first, Trollope works for me."

The 63 replies she received ranged from the instantly discounted "Have Viagra, will travel", and other unlikely-seeming pairings, to a pile of interest-sounding men.

Jane did indeed have a lot of sex with men she liked.

Initially intending to write her book as a novel, Jane tried running some of her early drafts past her writing group - of which she'd been a member for 20 years.

But rather than receiving constructive criticism, she was often met with an uncomfortable silence.

Then one of her lovers asked to see her work - she'd never hidden the fact that she was using her foray into promiscuity as fodder for a book.

He gave her two pieces of advice - leave the writing group, and write the book as non-fiction.

Despite having no connections in publishing, and no agent, Jane secured a book deal.

At the age of 67, she had achieved two goals she'd previously thought of as unlikely, and transformed her life in the process.

She managed it by refusing to accept that there is an age at which you have to accept your lot in life, and taking deliberate steps to shake things up.

There is no age at which you should just settle for the status quo.

In fact, the older you are, it's almost more important that you reinvent yourself if you feel the need.

The clock cannot be turned back, and you will always regret the things you didn't do more than the things you did[6].

So stop using age as an excuse for not improving your lot and start living.

[6] A team of researchers at Cornell University has found evidence for this during their Legacy Project http://legacyproject.human.cornell.edu/

Not my fault

Taking extreme ownership

"Responsibility does not only lie with the leaders of our countries or with those who have been appointed or elected to do a particular job. It lies with each one of us individually."

Tenzin Gyatso, the Dalai Lama

The US Navy SEALS have an infamous training programme called Hell Week.

Part of the training involves a race exercise with six boats, each with six crew. One person on each boat is the designated leader, responsible for the crew's performance.

The boats are large heavy inflatables which get heavier still once they fill with sand and water.

After an initial paddle through choppy Pacific Ocean waves, each boat team then has to carry the boat above them for miles on the beach, and then through a tough assault course, before returning to the ocean and finally finishing the course back on the beach.

All six crews have to do several races. Although the objective is to win, another is to avoid being last.

Jocko Willink and Leif Babin, in their book 'Extreme Ownership: How U.S. Navy SEALS Lead And Win', described observing one of these training exercises.

Boat II had a strong leader, and each of the crew seemed highly motivated and performed well, resulting in them winning most of the races.

Boat VI's performance was dismal, with them coming last in virtually every race, often lagging behind by a wide margin.

Boat VI's crew members bickered, argued and sniped at each other, accusing each other of under-performing.

Boat VI's leader seemed indifferent to his crew's poor performance, as if he had been unlucky to have been put in charge of a group of under-performers.

The Senior Chief of the exercise decided to swap the crew leaders of Boats II and VI.

In the next race, the first two boats were neck and neck.

Boat VI crossed the finishing line first, followed closely by Boat II in second place.

Boat VI had achieved an amazing turnaround, going from last to first.

In subsequent races, Boat II continued to challenge Boat VI, but narrowly lost most races to Boat VI.

Other than the leaders, these crews were the same.

Boat II's crew, as a result of their previous great leadership, had continued to work together well and already understood what they needed to do, which means they remained in the first two positions.

Boat VI's crew, which had previously been badly led, massively improved its performance to become a winner by having a great leader.

Willink and Babin describe it like this: "It was a glaring, undeniable example of the most fundamental and important truths at the heart of Extreme Ownership: there are no bad teams, only bad leaders."

MARIUS' LEGIONARIES AGREED TO BE
PACK MULES THEMSELVES?

Getting the culture right in your family, workplace or society has a lot to do with setting expectations around taking personal responsibility.

People often attribute the success of others to luck or circumstances, and therefore end up making excuses for their own failure, and for the failure of the people around them.

We can think our poor performance is down to just bad luck, or beyond our control, or because of poorly performing bosses or people - basically blaming anyone else but ourselves.

We fail to take ownership of things when they go wrong.

Take full responsibility for your current situation and for what you need to do to improve it.

Above all, become the leader you'd most like to follow.

Passive attack

One essential habit to cultivate your thinking and knowledge

"Reading is important, because if you can read, you can learn anything about everything and everything about anything."

Tomie dePaola, writer and illustrator

I grew up with my parents and three siblings in a tiny terraced house in London in the 1970s.

The house was cramped, cluttered and noisy.

Being a curious child I drove my mother mad with a barrage of questions about everything and anything.

When I was about 10 I found out that the local library remained open to 8pm on Mondays and Thursdays.

Problem solved!

For the next five years I would spend two hours every Monday and Thursday evening in the quiet of the library, with thousands of books at my fingertips.

I devoured books about space travel and the solar system, ecology and conservation, politics and economics, warfare and human conflicts, psychology and communication.

I read short stories, long stories, classic stories, thriller stories, crime stories, funny stories, plays and poems.

I must have read about 500 books by the time I was 16.

While I never really engaged in my school work and didn't pass many exams, I did leave school with all the knowledge that I'd gained from reading all those books in the library.

Without realising it I'd also taught myself a wide vocabulary, the principles of grammar and punctuation, and developed a deep level of comprehension.

I had broadened my perspective on a wide range of subjects and issues far beyond what I had learned at my 'comprehensive' school (a term which would be a candidate for prosecution under the Trade Descriptions Act if ever there was one).

But the most important skill that I developed during my evening visits to the library was a love of learning, and the ability to think for myself and question the status quo.

Greater knowledge provides a rich well from which you can draw to help stimulate new ideas, thinking and perspectives.

It can help you to devise strategy or to anticipate potential scenarios, as well as better able to handle any obstacles and setbacks.

The better informed you are, the more opportunities you'll spot, and the better your decision making is likely to be.

As well as your personal life experiences, reading is one of the most effective and efficient means of obtaining knowledge.

Unlike watching television or online videos, which are passive activities, research has shown that reading is a much more effective means of absorbing and understanding information.

And reading from paper books has been shown to be more effective than reading from electronic devices, because the typical person can read a printed page much faster than an electronic one.

Published books are also subject to much higher quality control over the content than much of what is written online.

Reading also causes your brain cells to burn about twice as many calories as it would normally, so learning new things can also help keep you trim as well!

But what should you be reading?

It is certainly possible to gain knowledge from reading fiction books - particularly those with lots of historical, scientific or economics detail - but non-fiction books are likely to provide the richest source of knowledge.

Reading a wide and diverse range of biographies, historical, military, political, personal development, philosophy, business, and psychology books is likely to yield the best knowledge 'return'.

Acquiring knowledge, however, requires effort and discipline. In our digital, hyper-connected, 'always on' world, it's easy to slip into lazy ways.

I'm saddened but not surprised when people tell me that they don't read books.

Publishers advise that few non-fiction books are read all the way through, with most readers giving up after about 80 pages.

I now read (carefully and thoroughly) about at least 50 paper books a year (I also listen to audio summaries of another 100 books each year).

Here is how I do it:

- I always have two new books 'in stock' so I am never without something to read.

- I maintain a 'wishlist' of new books, which I might purchase in the future, so I don't do impulse purchases.

- I only buy paper books, and always seek the cheapest net price for a nearly-new version (not always Amazon), on the basis that I don't require quick delivery or a new copy.

- Once a month I choose a book from my personal library to re-read, because it's amazing how much more you get from a second read.

- Every day I read at least 20 pages first thing in the morning, and at least 20 pages before I go to bed - this ensures that I can read 280 pages a week, which is about the size of most non-fiction books.

- If a book is longer than 280 pages, or I am particularly enjoying it, I read extra pages throughout the day, whenever I get a few minutes.

- I always read with a pencil and a pad of small coloured sticky notes, so I can mark interesting and important passages, making it easier for me to identify the location when I have finished the book.

Despite the Internet giving us all access to almost limitless amounts of information, it is only through the disciplined, regular and careful reading of quality paper books that meaningful and lasting knowledge is to be found.

If you've got out of the habit (or never had one) of reading books, then I suggest you start out slowly with a commitment to read at least one non-fiction book each month for three months.

Order three titles that interest you and which have good reviews.

Commit to reading a quarter of a book each week, which for a typical 300-page book is 75 pages a week.

Read each quarter of the book in five equal segments, over five days each week (you can have two days off), which is equivalent to 15 pages a day.

Read eight pages when you get up and another seven pages before you go to bed.

After three months, once you've developed the routine and habit of regular reading you can increase the number of pages you read each morning and night from seven or eight to 15, then 20, then 25, then 30.

By then you'll be reading one book a week and as a result building knowledge, confidence and useful insights.

So stop being passive watching the TV or surfing the internet, get reading!

Drains & radiators

Choose carefully who you have around you

"Surround yourself with only people who are going to lift you higher."

Oprah Winfrey, chat show host

Over the 25 years that I was in practice as a financial adviser, I conducted discovery interviews with several hundred people, where each told me their personal story.

I have also had the privilege to hear the personal stories of a similar number of professionals from the fields of financial planning, investment management, law and accounting.

On top of that I have read literally hundreds of biographies of political, business, scientific and charity leaders.

The common characteristic of the most successful people that I have met, and read about, is a surprisingly simple one - they choose carefully who they have around them.

Being intentional about the company you keep makes a lot of sense.

Some people are drains, and will sap your positive energy, while others are radiators, who can boost your ability to achieve.

If you are a squash player, you can't improve unless you play an opponent who is better than you, to make you raise your game.

If you employ people who don't have the right attitude or capability to do the work that you can't or don't want to do, you won't be able to delegate.

If your social circle is full of people who are pessimistic, negative, defeatist or cynical, then it will drag you down.

Whether it's a 'friend' that drags you down, an employee who can't perform, or a relative who is draining, either cut them out of your life or reduce their involvement in it.

Finding, cultivating and maintaining meaningful personal relationships with the right types of people is an essential activity that should be a priority for all those who want to live a meaningful, fulfilling and long life.

"YEAH SAMMY TOLD ME THAT I COULD PITCH THIS
AND EARN MY INTERFACE UPGRADE"

By all means seek out people with different backgrounds, education and opinions, but try to ensure that they are optimistic, positive, capable and excited about the future.

Clearly it is not possible to have deep relationships with more than a handful of people, but it is possible to develop meaningful, positive and supportive relationships with several hundred people, if you are intentional about it.

The easiest way to do this is to develop a mindset of giving rather than expecting to receive anything.

When the sale of my stake in my financial advice business went public, I was staggered by the number of positive, supportive and encouraging messages I received from people I had met over the years.

Some of these people I hadn't seen for a long time.

However, they felt compelled to contact me after hearing the news of my departure, often because of something they felt I had done for them.

Whether it was listening to their challenges, inspiring them to greater success, championing their profession, or sharing my own successes and failures (I've had plenty of both!), they felt a connection to me.

So have a think now about the company that you currently keep, and whether it is conducive to your own happiness and success.

When you've worked out who you really want in your life, have a think about what you can do for them, which they will value and appreciate.

Do this regularly and consistently, and your own happiness and success will be assured.

A friend in need

Learn and teach by ex-ample

"The world is changed by your example, not by your opinion."

Paulo Coelho, lyricist and novelist

When I was 26 I met David, a brilliant and successful financial planner in his mid 40s.

David epitomised all the values, principles and approach to life that I believe in.

As well as being a total professional, he was a lovely person who seemed to bring out the best in everyone with whom he came into contact.

David was always encouraging, supportive and enthusiastic towards me and my career.

Over the years he sent me a number of handwritten notes of encouragement and acknowledgement of things I had done well.

He would give me book recommendations and freely share his knowledge and insights.

David was always available to speak to me on the telephone, whenever I needed advice, help or encouragement.

The amazing thing about David was that he bothered to spend any of his valuable time with me, when he was clearly a very wealthy and busy man with lots of things on his plate.

David died suddenly at the age of 54 in 2005, and I still miss him to this day.

But I still remember his wise words of wisdom, and I attribute much of my success to his influence as a positive role model and mentor, and for that I am very grateful.

While it's important to avoid idolising or putting people on a pedestal – Steve Jobs, for example, was notoriously nasty and aggressive towards people – if you find people that you admire, you can explore what, why and how they work, to find clues as to what might help you achieve similar outcomes.

A good role model should be someone who you can look to as a good example of who you want to be like.

A mentor, on the other hand, is someone with whom you have a personal relationship, who offers guidance, advice and a sounding board for your ideas.

In addition to David, I'm fortunate to have had several other great role models and mentors in my life, that I admired and from whom I have gained inspiration, wisdom and encouragement to help me to become the person I am today.

Most successful and happy people I have met or read about have also had role models and mentors at some stage in their lives.

Finding a mentor is likely to be one of the most productive and meaningful ways of achieving the personal and business outcomes you desire, because it is a very personal and relevant approach.

The best mentors often have their own mentors, because they are generally the type of people who have made a commitment to life-long personal improvement.

When I decided to become a professional speaker, I hired Alan Stevens[7] as my speaking mentor.

We met each month and spoke on the phone in between.

Alan's guidance, advice and support helped me to develop the confidence, skills and knowledge to build my speaking career far quicker than might have been the case had I struggled along on my own.

I also made a good friend.

Being a mentor to others is also a highly rewarding experience.

Research has shown that being of service to others releases dopamine to the brain, the hormone which gives us a feeling of well-being and happiness.

One entrepreneur I know makes available 30 minutes a day, free of charge, to provide ongoing and one-off mentoring to aspiring entrepreneurs.

[7] www.mediacoach.co.uk

I enjoy mentoring younger people.

Far from me coming up with all the answers, I ask the tough questions that help the person I'm mentoring to come up with their own answers and make their own decisions.

It's very gratifying to see someone develop and grow their capability and multiply their success.

So how about you?

Do you have the right people around you?

Or could your experience and knowledge help someone else develop and grow?

Give it up

Why you need to make other people look good

Melissa was in a fairly senior management position, but she wasn't enjoying her job.

A few years previously she'd moved to Toronto from the UK, because her husband is Canadian.

So there she was in a new city, in a new home, with no friends, and she wasn't enjoying her job. She was feeling that the whole thing had been a big mistake.

It didn't help that her boss was very chaotic and didn't seem to know what her priorities were or should be.

Rather than give attitude back, get defensive, or become annoyed, Melissa decided to do everything to serve her boss and make her look really good to the board of directors.

Every single day that was Melissa's mission - to make her boss look good.

And she never once drew attention to it; she never once tried to get any recognition for what she was doing.

Melissa just put all her energy into helping her boss get her own priorities sorted.

And, as time went by, Melissa got promotions and pay raises that she didn't even apply for.

She's a director now in that same company. Had she not focused on making her boss look good, she'd probably have ended up quitting and going for a similar position elsewhere, without the same kind of opportunities.

"CAN YOU STOP MAKING ME LOOK GOOD?
MY PARTNERS HAVE BEEN ADVISING ME TO
PROMOTE YOU"

If you think like a victim you'll never achieve your potential in the face of setbacks, adversity and failures.

If you think like a victor, and take responsibility for your situation, you'll be able to bounce back and prosper.

Making other people look good is an essential attribute to cultivate.

The more you help other people to improve, advance, and receive well-deserved recognition, the happier and more effective you'll become.

Run your own race

Compare your present to your progress not your peers

"If you compare yourself with others, you may become vain or bitter, for always there will be greater and lesser persons than yourself."

Desiderata, Max Ehrmann

Over the years I've entered quite a few running races.

I see some runners get carried away with the race atmosphere and go off too fast, only to crash out with a stitch after a few kilometres.

I see others trying to keep up with their friends and in the process hate the race experience from start to finish.

I prefer to focus on maintaining my target running pace in line with trying to beat my previous best time.

In that sense I am not particularly bothered what the other runners are doing.

I just put one foot after another and focus on my pace.

This means I have to accept that some runners will overtake me and that's OK because I'm focusing on my personal best.

As I mentioned earlier in Drains & radiators (p.41), during my career as a financial adviser I interviewed several hundred people and heard their life stories.

Looking back, my impression is that only a small proportion of these people were successful in the sense that they were truly happy, fulfilled and financially secure.

Some were wealthy, but had poor health due to lifestyle.

Others had many achievements to their name, but were unhappy.

Some worked hard, but never seemed to see the financial success which they were striving for.

Others seemed happy, but went through relationships like I get through running shoes.

What I have learned from these interviews, and my own life experiences, is that you can only be truly happy and successful when you stop judging yourself against other people.

Particularly today, with social media enabling people to constantly communicate a curated version of their 'perfect' life, it's even easier to fall into the peer comparison trap.

There will always be someone who is wealthier, taller, more attractive, wittier, thinner, better connected, luckier, fitter, and smarter than you.

Constant improvement, yes.

Living your life constantly in the shadow of others, no.

Self-acceptance sounds simple, but I know from personal experience that it is one of the hardest things to do, particularly if you are entrepreneurial or a high-achiever.

Spending money to impress others is a fool's errand.

Creating a façade of what you think will impress people or make them like you is too much hard work.

Comparing yourself to others is a recipe for unhappiness, destructive behaviour and burn-out.

Be honest with yourself - are you living your life through others?

Are you overly sensitive to what they think of you, how they live, their values and their achievements?

Being the best version of you is much more empowering than being the 'best'.

You can't be the best in everything, it's not possible, and to try to do that is to set yourself up to fail.

But that doesn't mean you should give up entirely; you can be the best in something.

Stop beating yourself up, find your 'thing', and do your best.

Learning to focus on achieving your personal best - and being true to your own ideals and values - is the foundation to true success.

It's far better to aim to be the best version of you, and run your own race, than be a fake version of someone else.

The funny thing is that the more you do this the happier, fulfilled and wealthier you'll become.

A penny for your thoughts

The simplest way to be present, connected and at peace

"The primary cause of unhappiness is never the situation, but your thoughts about it. Be aware of the thoughts you are thinking."

Eckhart Tolle, author

Over the course of my career as a financial adviser I must have carried out nearly 1,000 initial meetings with potential clients and conducted about 4,000 meetings in total, taking into account existing clients whom I advised over many years.

As you'd expect each of these people had a different life story, different circumstances and different hopes, dreams and goals.

But the biggest difference between them was in the way that they perceived their life and the world around them.

Some of them were very happy and fulfilled, while others seemed less so, despite having similar wealth, health, and opportunities.

When experiencing a setback, disappointment or failure, some of these people responded as if it was the end of the world, while others seemed unfazed and unconcerned.

Some people seemed very worried about what other people thought of them, while others couldn't care less.

My experience of meeting all these people has convinced me that the main difference between those who are happy, fulfilled and success-ful is how they respond to their daily random thoughts.

Most of us confuse our thoughts for who we are but we are wrong.

As Michael Neill explains in his book 'The Space Within': "Just because you have a thought in your head, it doesn't mean that it's your thought. It doesn't mean it's true, and it doesn't mean that it's actually what you think. It just means there's a thought in your head."

You don't need to hold on to thoughts, you don't need to push them out.

They do not define who you are.

Rather than trying to make sense of all these random thoughts and the emotional effort which that requires, it's better to accept that thoughts come and go and that it's OK.

Once you learn to accept that thoughts are random and constant, you can learn to be more present and live in the moment.

The more you can be present and in the moment, the more you can connect emotionally with other people.

The more you connect emotionally with others, the more you develop empathy, understanding and acceptance.

Your life is the sum of human interactions and personal relationships that you develop, and they'll be better, deeper and more meaningful if you can stop letting thoughts define who you are.

Thoughts are just thoughts, not the person you really are.

P'd off?

Follow this rule to avoid becoming frustrated

"The essence of being human is that one does not seek perfection."

George Orwell, author

About 10 years ago I felt frustrated and annoyed with myself.

I was frustrated that I hadn't achieved more with my life, and annoyed that I had let this happen.

At about the same time I joined an entrepreneurial coaching program with The Strategic Coach organisation.

One of the things they taught me was the concept of seeking progress, not perfection.

My frustration was caused by comparing my present situation to a perfect ideal in my head.

Seeking perfection is a recipe for disaster because it's an unattainable goal and you will just end up disappointed, beat yourself up and undermine your confidence.

Instead of comparing our present to an unattainable ideal - perfection - we were advised to compare our current position with our situation 10 years previously.

In my own case I was amazed to realise how much progress I had achieved in that time - health, wealth, professional achievements, friendships and life experiences.

Seeing how much progress I had achieved gave me two things: a renewed sense of confidence in my abilities, and optimism for what I could achieve in the future.

You can get really excited about having a future which is bigger and better than your past, by looking at the progress you have made over the past five, 10, 15 or 20 years.

So next time you feel frustrated or annoyed with your current situation remember: progress not perfection!

Eating an elephant

Big achievements made easy

"The man who moves a mountain begins by carrying away small stones."

Confucius, Chinese philosopher

Many years ago I had to take a really difficult investment management examination to achieve a professional qualification.

Passing the examination was very important, because without it I would no longer have been allowed to carry out my job.

I ordered the study material, which duly arrived in a rather ominus looking large box.

I unpacked the box to find several folders of study material, examination papers, packs of fact cards and a large reference book.

As I looked at this massive pile of material I felt so completely overwhelmed I almost felt like crying.

The task ahead of me seemed so immense I just didn't know where to start - let alone learn everything I needed to pass the exam!

After thinking carefully I realised that I had to break the task down into a series of smaller, more manageable steps over the weeks leading up to the exam.

Rather than focus on the entire task ahead of me, I looked at it as a number of weekly assignments to complete in isolation.

"WELL I THOUGHT GIVING HIM MORE CARROTS WOULD DO THE TRICK"

This enabled me to reduce my anxiety about getting all the study completed, as I focused on each week's activity.

Life is sometimes like studying for an exam.

You have a challenge, issue, task, project or situation to handle and you feel like you'll never complete it.

The key is to envisage what the ideal outcome looks like and how you'll feel when you've completed it, then break it down into more manageable chunks, each with their own target completion date.

Then just focus on completing each task in order, without thinking about the remaining tasks.

A new dawn

How to make more time

"We must use time wisely and forever realize that the time is always ripe to do right."

Nelson Mandela, former President of South Africa

Robin Sharma is a best-selling author, self-improvement coach, and entrepreneur.

Each day Sharma rises at 5am and he spends 20 minutes doing light exercise, 20 minutes writing and reviewing his journal, and 20 minutes meditating.

This special hour, before most people are up, allows Sharma to focus on getting his mind right so he can have a happy, productive and enjoyable day.

"Get up early. I dare you to do it for a few weeks. Your life is too precious a thing to waste. You know you were meant for your own unique form of greatness. You know you can do more, have more and be more. You know that you can be bigger than you currently are. So join The 5 O'Clock Club. Win The Battle of The Bed. Put mind over mattress. Get up early. And as Benjamin Franklin once noted: 'There will be plenty of time to sleep when you are dead'."

Here are Robin's five practical tactics to help you get up early[8]:

1. **Don't eat after 7pm.** You will sleep more deeply as well as more sweetly. It's the quality not the quantity of sleep that's most important.

2. **Don't lounge in bed after your alarm clock goes off.** Jump out of bed and start your day. The more time you lie in bed after the alarm clock goes off, the greater the likelihood that the chatter of your mind will say something like, 'Stay in bed. Sleep a bit more. You deserve it.'

3. **Get into world-class physical condition.** When I am in excellent physical shape – working out five or six times a week and eating ultra-well, I jump out of bed at 5am or even 4am with ease. Being superbly fit is a brilliant move.

4. **Set BHAGs.** Jim Collins coined the term 'BHAGs', meaning Big Hairy Audacious Goals. Goals breathe life and energy into your days. Goals inspire you and give you something to get out of bed for each morning. Taking out your journal and articulating 10, five, three and one year goals for the core dimensions of your life will focus your mind and drive tremendous results. It will light a fire in your belly and flood you with passion.

5. **Set your alarm clock 30 minutes early.**

So if you want to become super productive, mentally and physically strong, and generally get more out of life, go to bed and get up a bit earlier.

---

[8] Taken from www.robinsharma.com/blog/06/be-wise-early-rise/ Reproduced by permission.

Getting up at 5am might be a bit too extreme at the outset.

I suggest that you start out small, perhaps 20 minutes earlier every day for a few weeks, and then extend that by another 20 minutes, and then another, until you are rising at least an hour earlier every day.

Don't worry if you fall off the wagon and slip into your old waking habits at some stage.

Just re-commit to waking earlier the next day, and do so until it becomes a habit.

Self
sabotage

The enemy lurking in
your life or business

My friend David runs a very successful financial services business.

A few years ago he started finding
that some new employees were
not settling into their role very well,
and as a result were not being as
productive as they needed to be.

They even had to terminate some
staff who just couldn't seem to get
to grips with the work.

David asked his business manager, who handled the staff hiring, to
review their hiring process and find
out why things were going wrong.

The business manager reported back, and David found that a
critical step - of putting candidates
through an online personality assessment - was not being carried
out.

The business manager had thought
that her own assessment skills
were good enough, and that by not
having candidates do the test, she
was saving the company money.
But by not doing the test, the business manager was not filtering out

people whose personalities were not suitable for the roles. This was, ironically, costing the company money.

Once the test was reinstated in the hiring process, the success rate of new employees increased significantly.

Most people, me included, find that at some stage in their life they engage in self-sabotage.

The thing about self-sabotage is that we don't know we are doing it.

We have the best intentions, but...

For some reason we stop doing what worked in the past.

Or we start making things too complicated when they don't need to be.

"NO, I ASSURE YOU, THE DELUXE ONION CUTTER 2000 WILL BE BETTER"

Sometimes we stick with doing things like we always have, even though it is clear that times have changed and we need to do things differently.

Or we unwittingly change a process, procedure or routine which re-sults in the outcome not being as good as it could be.

Self-sabotage might even take the form of accepting indiscretions each day, such as failing to be polite.

In my experience, other than perhaps some people with mental health issues, no-one sets out to engage in self-sabotage.

So if things aren't going right in a particular aspect at home or work, think carefully about whether you or anyone else is engaged in self-sabotage, and put it right.

Cancelling the space shuttle

When you need to sacrifice sacred cows

"If you can't fly then run, if you can't run then walk, if you can't walk then crawl, but whatever you do you have to keep moving forward."

Martin Luther King Jr, civil rights activist

In the same year that man walked on the moon, President Nixon of the United States authorised the start of exploratory work into the development of a reusable manned spacecraft.

In 1972 the US Congress approved funding for the Space Shuttle programme, with the first manned flight occurring nearly 10 years later in April 1981.

The original intention was that the Shuttle would be used to help construct and supply the new International Space Station until the mid-1990s, by when it was expected NASA would have developed the next generation of reusable manned spacecraft, to enable missions to Mars and beyond.

But the service life of the Shuttle was extended several times until it was finally retired 30 years later in 2011, at least 15 years longer than originally planned.

Since the Space Shuttle programme ended, NASA has not had

its own means of launching cargo or people into space, and currently relies on the Russian Soyuz spacecraft to take its astronauts to the International Space Station and either Space X or the European Space Agency to launch its satellites.

NASA expects (or hopes) to have its next manned spacecraft ready in 2018, over seven years after the retirement of the shuttle.

The Shuttle programme is a good example of a problem that many people and organisations face - just continuing with what they know.

It's easier to maintain the status quo, working with what's familiar, sticking with the tried and tested.

The problem with this approach is that it can lull you into a false sense of security, and you don't have either the need or resources (time and money) to develop new ideas, capabilities and opportunities.

"I'LL WAKE YOU UP WHEN IT'S BROKEN"

If NASA had retired the Shuttle in the late 1990s, they'd have had a serious need to develop a next-generation manned spacecraft and would have therefore freed up the resources to make it happen.

Think about what activities, projects and initiatives you are holding onto in your life or business, which are no longer appropriate for you now, and which you really should retire to make room for new ideas, projects and priorities.

The last thing you want to do is to keep soldiering on with out-of-date ideas and find out that life has passed you by and you're out of the game for seven years - like NASA.

Less is more

The power of simple

"Simple can be harder than complex. You have to work hard to get your thinking clean to make it simple. But it's worth it in the end, because once you get there, you can move mountains."

Steve Jobs, founder of Apple Inc.

In my financial services firm we developed lots of processes, checklists and protocols for every activity in the business to ensure we were efficient, consistent and thorough.

When we worked with a new client, after the initial consultations and gathering of personal information, we progressed to a stage which covered a first look at their overall financial situation.

The checklist for preparing, carrying out and following up on this initial planning assessment meeting had about 45 steps, and took many hours of work by several members of staff.

The meeting itself involved lots of printed paper reports, lists, and other documents that were felt to be relevant to the meeting.

One of these documents was a draft financial planning report with lots of pretty charts and other graphics.

One day I read a quotation by the 20th century French writer Antoine de Saint-Exupery in which he said: "You know you have achieved perfection in design, not when you have nothing more to add, but when you have nothing more to take away."

This motivated me to sit down and look carefully at a print-out of the checklist and ask myself this question: "How many steps, actions, documents and tasks can we remove from this process to improve the experience and outcome for our clients?"

Why create a draft plan beforehand, when we can easily and quickly do it with the client in the meeting, and show them the outputs on the wall-mounted monitor?

That would remove eight steps from the process.

Then we'd not need to wait to gather all the client's data before the meeting, because we could get that from the client when they were with us - five fewer steps in the process.

Then we'd not need to check and print out the paper draft plan report for the meeting - two fewer steps in the process.

In fact, why print out any paper before the meeting when we could easily and quickly print out a hard copy if the client wanted it?

And why were we writing up long-form minutes of the meeting when a short bulleted summary, together with a recording of the meeting, would be quicker and easier to produce?

I took a coloured marker pen and started crossing through several of the checklist steps and modifying others.

I ended up with a much shorter, quicker and more efficient draft planning checklist, and a meeting experience which was more engaging, collaborative and interactive for the client.

I then presented my suggestions to the team to get their thoughts.

Everyone agreed that it was a major improvement both for the team and the clients, and had all secretly felt that the process was more complicated than it needed to be.

After a few weeks the time spent planning, holding and following up on these meetings reduced by about 60%.

We then applied the same thinking to review meetings with existing clients, and achieved a similar outcome.

We then started applying the same logic to all the other checklists, and after about a year we had transformed our productivity, staff happiness, accuracy and client satisfaction levels.

"NOW WE JUST HAVE TO FIND WHERE WE
STARTED, THEN WE CAN SHOW IT TO THE CLIENT"

We are all guilty of overcomplicating things in our lives at some stage.

Just because you've always done something a certain way for a long time, don't suffer in silence, ask the question "how could we improve this to make it simpler?"

Simple isn't easy, but it's essential if you want to get the most out of anything.

Simple forces you to distill things down to their essential parts.

Make it simple and move your own mountains.

Talk is cheap

Why proactivity is key

In the early years of my financial advice business, when I had no budget for marketing, I decided to write a guide.

I called the guide 'How to be your own financial adviser'.

I mailed the guide to about 20 personal finance journalists who worked for the major newspapers.

My friends couldn't understand why I was bothering to write a guide showing people how to be their own financial adviser, when my business was giving financial advice.

I followed up with calls to each of the journalists to whom I had mailed a copy of the guide.

Some were unavailable, others weren't interested, but one - at the Financial Times - was.

This journalist explained that he was working on an article about how successful people felt emotionally about money in general and their personal finances in particular.

As I had included insights into emotions and money in my guide, the journalist was keen to include my ideas and comments in his article.

The following weekend, on the front page of the money section of the Financial Times, appeared his article - 'Lie down you're feeling wealthy' - with extensive comments from me on the role of emotions in managing money.

That exposure for my business was a pivotal turning point, and laid the basis for our future growth and success.

Regardless of what resources you have available, no matter how strong your competitors, or how hard life might be, you must take the initiative.

Put your ideas into action, follow people up, connect with people, try new ways of doing things, ask for help.

Above all if you want to be successful at anything in life you need to be proactive.

Coulda shoulda woulda

How one word can make a difference

I've never taken drugs or smoked cigarettes.

Like many people, however, I do drink alcohol.

My relationship with alcohol is very much love-hate.

I love savouring the taste and the pleasant feeling of relaxation that comes from a nice glass of wine.

But I hate the feeling of losing control, waking up in the middle of the night, or feeling groggy and sluggish the next day after drinking too much.

I've never been a daytime or weekday drinker, but some time ago I realised that my weekend alcohol consumption, while certainly not heavy, had gradually increased over the years to a level that I felt was not good for me.

I kept telling myself that I should drink less, but I never seemed to achieve a meaningful reduction.

83

This went on for quite some time, and I started feeling quite frustrated and annoyed with myself.

I didn't want to become teetotal, but I did want to reduce my alcohol consumption.

Then one day I said to myself that I *could* drink less if I wanted to.

That one word - could - made a massive difference.

JOE DIDN'T CARE, HE FINALLY STARTED CYCLING - TEMPORARILY IN THE WAY HE WANTED IT

Instead of the feelings of failure, pressure, obligation or expectation that are associated with should, I had feelings of hope, opportunity, possibility and choice associated with the word *could*.

Using this simple strategy enabled me to reduce my alcohol consumption by two-thirds overnight.

Now I enjoy a few glasses of wine a few days a week, without a detrimental impact on my physical or mental health.

So, think about saying to yourself you *could* do something rather than you should.

Now I'll raise a glass to that!

The secret to daily happiness

The mindset you need to be happy each day

When I was a teenager I got a weekend job at the local pub.

My job involved getting the bar ready for the busy Saturday and Sunday trade.

On my first day Ken, the owner of the pub, showed me how to do each of the tasks I was required to carry out.

He showed me how to clean the toilets, restock the shelves and optics, and tidy the cellar.

He showed me how to empty the big bins of empty bottles into their relevant crates, water the hanging baskets correctly, and clean the filters on the glass-washing machines.

Finally, he showed me how to clean the cellar steps.

First they had to be thoroughly swept.

Then they needed to be scrubbed hard with soapy water and a stiff hand brush.

Then they needed wiping down with a towel until they were spotless.

I asked Ken why we needed to clean the cellar steps so well when few people would ever see them, and when they would only get dirty again.

Ken replied: "At least four of the bar staff will come down the cellar over the course of the weekend and they will see the cellar steps. They will see the pride and care with which these steps have been cleaned, and they'll take that standard with them when they go back into the bar."

"But, more importantly, you'll know that when you've finished work, in addition to your wages, you'll have the happiness that comes from the pride of having done your best to leave the pub in the best possible condition."

Ken's advice really struck a chord with me, and contrasts with Steve Jobs' advice in his commencement speech to the graduating class of Stanford University in 2005.

Jobs advised students to only do a job that they were passionate about, on the basis that they would spend a lot of time at work, and that this would make them happy.

It's great if you can do a job you're passionate about, but what if you can't?

In the real world many people can't do a job that they're passionate about, at least not 100% of the time, and this is particularly true for many young people at the beginning of their working lives.

If you are only happy doing a job that you are passionate about, but can't find that perfect job, then you're destined to be unhappy a lot of the time.

Having pride in a job well done, no matter how mundane, routine or unseen, can give a sense of self-reward and contentment each day, even if that job is not something you're passionate about.

So even if your job isn't something you'd describe as a 'passion', you can find the positives and do the job well, and win every day.

You're not getting ready for some great big day where it's all going to be wonderful and perfect; life is the sum of your daily experiences.

Knowing the cellar steps in the pub were spotless, and that I'd done all the other jobs well, did give me a sense of pride and that made me happy every day that I worked in the pub.

Even with the most unglamorous jobs, if you take pride in what you do - whether or not anyone else acknowledges it - you can derive pleasure and satisfaction, which will make you happy every day.

What'd ya say?

The role that effective communication plays in your success

"Communication is a skill that you can learn. It's like riding a bicycle or typing. If you're willing to work at it, you can rapidly improve the quality of every part of your life."

Brian Tracy, author of The Psychology of Achievement

For the past few years I've carried out mock interviews for sixth-formers at my daughter's school.

One of the questions I ask the students is, "How are you at handling difficult situations?"

Sometimes I go on to ask how they'd tackle telling a colleague that they have a body odour problem.

Nobody wants to tell anyone they have a B.O. problem.

One girl who I was interviewing came up with an excellent answer.

She said, "The way I'd do it would be to bring it up in a general sense, in a group setting with a bit of humour, and tell a story about someone I know - maybe someone at my dad's firm - who had to speak to a colleague about a similar problem."

I said, "That's not really raising the issue, is it?"

But she hadn't finished. "I'd do that first of all," she continued.

"Then after a week or two, if the penny hadn't dropped, then I'd take them aside and have a quiet word, referring to the story I told and explaining that I'd had some complaints."

For an 18 year old, that's a smart, empathetic solution; raising the topic generally to see if there's any acceptance.

Much of happiness and success in life comes down to communication.

Most marriage failures happen because of lack of communication.

Most business relationship breakdowns happen because of lack of communication.

"SIR , MADAM, THERE'S A PUT-YOUR-PHONES-AWAY POLICY FOR DATING COUPLES HERE"

You might ask someone to do something, perhaps a supplier, a colleague, a friend, or even a spouse, and you get complete radio silence.

Because you don't know what's going on you have to make assumptions.

They might very well be on top of the situation, but you won't know that because they haven't told you, and you think they don't care.

The first rule of being a better communicator is to bear in mind that people have very different personalities and prefer to communicate in very different ways.

For example, I like short emails or reports in bullet point form with a clear point of action, but my employees used to send me long, complicated emails.

They would also often ask me lots of questions, but failed to realise that everyone else was doing the same, and I only had so much time to give answers.

Eventually my colleagues learned to send me emails with brief information and only a few questions.

This understanding led to improved communications.

You can become a more effective communicator by gaining an awareness of how you come across to other people, how they come across to you, different learning styles, how different times of the day affect different people, and crucially, knowing things like when you actually need to pick up the phone to someone rather than send an email.

It's not just about what you communicate to others, either.

How many times have you gone to an event, whether a conference, party or other gathering, you have a conversation with someone and you get a sense that they're not properly listening?

And you know this because they're digging in their pocket for their phone, or getting a slightly glazed look as they wait for you to finish your sentence so they can say something.

Becoming a brilliant communicator is just as much about listening as it is about speaking.

They'll also pay attention to body language since not all communication is verbal. Holding eye contact is very important, in particular.

The point is you don't have to be perfect, you just have to try to be a better communicator , one person at a time.

The victorious loser

Why failing is essential to success

In the late 1950s the United States and the Soviet Union (now known as Russia) were in a race to be the first country to put a man in space and bring him back safely.

Billions of dollars were spent, thousands of bright people were employed, and enormous resources were deployed in each country's space program.

Success was seen as a point of national pride, with the winner able to stake a claim of scientific, intellectual and engineering excellence.

In April 1961 Yuri Gagarin of the Soviet Union became the first human to go into space.

Although the Americans were the first to have a man orbit the earth in 1962, they had been beaten to the main prize by the Soviets.

While many Americans were shocked, embarrassed and annoyed at being beaten, President John F. Kennedy didn't see it that way.

In September 1962, President Kennedy gave a speech in which he committed the United States to sending a man to the moon and bringing him back safely to earth again before the decade was out.

In a few short minutes the President had set out a goal which was bigger, bolder, and far more ambitious than anyone was considering, less than 18 months after the Soviets had put the first man into space.

NASA, the United States' space agency, had a renewed purpose and focus, and they galvanised all the country's resources around this single objective, with less than eight years to achieve it.

As we all know, Neil Armstrong was the first man to walk on the moon in 1969, which eclipsed the Soviets' earlier achievement by a wide margin.

The United States had pulled off the amazing, incredible feat of a successful moon landing because their president decided to use their earlier defeat as a catalyst for a bigger achievement.

When you suffer a setback, disappointment or failure in your life, which makes you despondent, upset or disillusioned, and considering conceding defeat or giving up, don't.

Follow President Kennedy's example and be bolder, more ambitious in your goals, and renew your determination to achieve them.

To be of service

Understanding who your customer is

"Never lose sight of the fact that the most important yardstick of your success will be how you treat other people - your family,- friends, and coworkers, and even strangers you meet along the way."

Barbara Bush, former First Lady of the United States

In addition to being a writer I speak professionally on a regular basis.

When I do a keynote speech my customer is the organiser who booked me, the one who signed my engagement letter and is going to authorise the payment.

It's been her job to find a speaker who'll offer value to the delegates, so I want to make her look good by fulfilling that role.

But as important as she is to me, the organiser is not my only customer.

Obviously the delegates are my customers because they will provide feedback to the organiser about whether I delivered value.

I also think about the people in charge of the audio visual equipment as my customers because if I make them feel good about working with me, they're going to be positive about me if anyone asks about potential speakers.

Other speakers at the same event are also my customers, because they're likely to be sitting and listening to me along with the delegates.

I want them to think well of me, and maybe pass on my details when they hear that someone's looking for a speaker at another event.

The venue's staff are also my customers, because they run such events all the time and might be asked to recommend speakers.

So my customers are a much wider group than you might at first think, and they represent a network of potential contacts.

The point is you have to widen your scope over who you think of as your customers.

Your customers are also your colleagues, your boss, your subordinates, your suppliers, anyone who's got anything to do with your 'to do' list.

But this isn't just a work-related issue.

Your family, your friends and relatives are all your customers.

They all give you something, and you give them something in return, whether that's money, time, advice, support, love or anything else for that matter.

If you only think that a customer is someone you sell something to for economic gain, whether it's a product or a service, then you're setting yourself a very limited potential for value creation.

If you can create significant value for lots of people, then your own life satisfaction will be assured.

That's why it pays to consider that everyone is your customer.

"I WOULD ALSO LIKE TO THANK THE CARPENTERS
WITHOUT THEM THERE WOULD BE NO PLATFORM
FOR ME TO STAND ON TODAY"

Risk it for the Triscuit

Learning to embrace and leverage risk

US biscuit manufacturer Nabisco once ran a particularly memorable advertising campaign for its Triscuit brand.

The campaign revolved around the idea that people who would do anything for this kind of wheat-based cracker.

The adverts showed people engaging in dangerous acts simply to be able to consume the snack.

As a result, the phrase 'risk it for the Triscuit' became American slang for taking extreme risks for little reward.

In any aspect of life, this isn't something you want to be doing.

However, that's not to say that risk should be avoided.

John Paul Jones, the US naval commander, said: "It seems to be a law of nature, inflexible and inexorable, that those who will not risk cannot win."

What's important is to only take *calculated* risks, where there is a good chance of adequate reward or compensation.

For example, say I want to cross the road.

If I choose to cross a road with very little traffic, during the day, at a clearly marked pedestrian crossing and I look and listen carefully, the chances of me being involved in an accident are extremely low.

On the other hand, if I choose to cross a very busy road, at night, while listening to music and looking at my smartphone, the chances of me being involved in an accident increase significantly.

That being said, an accident isn't inevitable. Taking the higher risk is all well and good but it only makes sense if the reward is high enough to compensate.

In both cases, the reward I get is the same — I cross the road.

But what about if the risky crossing helps me avoid a three-mile walk to the pedestrian crossing, and means I can watch the recording of an important business meeting so I can be prepared for my next appointment?

You should only take those risks which you need to take and which have a high chance of being compensated in the form of a better outcome.

Many people take risks they don't need to take.

For example, investing in risky stock market investments in old age as part of an inheritance tax planning scheme.

But on the flip side some people don't take enough risk, and as a result don't always live the lifestyle that they might.

THE HIRING MANAGER HAS CALCULATED THE RISKS,
THE NEW GUY DID NOT HAVE ANY EXPERIENCES, BUT
AT LEAST HE HAD A GOOD PORTFOLIO

For example, a few years ago I was counselling a newly retired married couple.

I showed them that they would be financially secure under every conceivable scenario, and that they could afford to live a bit before they got too old.

A key short-term goal was a six-week trip to Australia and New Zealand, which they were planning to fly economy class.

I tried to convince them to fly from London in business class, to have a better experience than 23 hours of sitting in economy.

They could easily afford it, but they just didn't think they could, or should.

A few months later I received an email from the couple, with a picture of them drinking Champagne in business class on their flight to Australia.

All the message said was "See, we did take your advice!" They certainly didn't have any regrets.

Sometimes you do have to risk it for the Triscuit.

Hairy & scary

Being bold about long-term goals

Zhang Xin was born in Beijing, China in the 1960s, and grew up in a faceless communal housing estate.

Following the separation of her parents Zhang, aged 14, moved with her mother to Hong Kong, where they shared a dingy single room flat.

For the next five years Zhang toiled in a succession of small factories, making garments and electronics, to save enough money to travel to England.

Aged 19, Zhang arrived in England and studied English at a secretarial school.

With the help of scholarships and grants, she went on to study economics at Sussex University, followed by a Master's degree at Cambridge University.

Following graduation, Zhang was hired by investment bank Goldman Sachs in Hong Kong.

In 1995, she met her future husband and together they founded a property development company which is now called SOHO China.

Zhang and her husband grew SOHO China into the largest developer in Beijing and Shanghai.

In 2014 Forbes magazine listed Zhang as the 62nd most powerful woman in the world.

In 2015, her net worth was estimated to be US$3.6B.

What makes Zhang's story so incredible is not the level of wealth or influence that she has created, but the fact that she was so determined to improve her life through hard work and education.

Unlike other young women in China and Hong Kong, Zhang was not prepared to accept that her life would remain drab, dreary and poor.

Zhang had a clear goal to improve her life and put all her energy into making that a reality.

It's highly likely that you will have more advantages available to you now than Zhang did when she was young.

The key question is whether your life goals are hairy and scary enough to motivate you to do what it takes to achieve them.

Most people overestimate what they can achieve in the short-term, but underestimate what they can achieve in a lifetime.

Set big hairy, scary long-term goals, and be realistic about what you can achieve over the next year.

SEEMS LIKE MARTHA'S PET GECKO HAS
DREAMS TO STAR IN HOLLYWOOD

The lone voice

Going against consensus

"Conformity is the jailer of freedom and the enemy of growth."

John F. Kennedy, former President of the United States

When I was a financial adviser, one of the services we provided for our clients was creating and managing individual investment portfolios.

To create these portfolios we used a number of investment funds from several of the large investment management providers.

We then monitored the portfolios and made adjustments as necessary to ensure that they remained allocated to the correct funds, as their values changed over time.

We had also been collecting and paying over to the tax authorities Value Added Tax (VAT) of 20% on our annual monitoring fees, which was in line with accepted opinion and practice.

One day I had a look at the tax rules to confirm for myself that our fees were in fact subject to VAT.

VAT rules are fiendishly complex and I filled up several pages of A3 paper with diagrams, flow charts and lists of all the relevant rules.

After several hours I came to the conclusion that our fees were not subject to VAT.

I shared my findings with our tax adviser and he agreed that my analysis did suggest that VAT might not be payable on our fees, but that it wasn't a clear-cut case.

We applied to the tax authority to have a refund of tax we had previously paid over the past four years, and advised that we would not be paying VAT in the future.

The tax authority assigned a tax inspector to investigate our claim.

The tax inspector eventually wrote to us to say that we were required to pay VAT and that they would not give a refund.

We asked for the inspector's decision to be formally reviewed by a more senior inspector.

The senior inspector agreed with the first inspector's opinion.

We therefore made an application to take the tax authority to a special court called the First Tier Tax Tribunal, which examines and adjudicates on disputes between taxpayers and the tax authority.

Eventually we ended up in court to put the facts of our case to the tribunal judge and his technical assistant, and explained why we didn't think we were liable to pay VAT on our fees, and as such were entitled to a refund of past tax.

A few months later we received the judge's written ruling.

The judge agreed that we were not liable to pay VAT on our investment monitoring fees and as such were also due a refund from the past four years - we had won.

We received a very significant repayment from the tax authorities which we used to make large reductions in our future fees, so that all our clients benefited from the outcome.

Our case was big news in both the accounting profession and the financial services sector, because it confirmed that consensus opinion and practice was in fact wrong.

It's easy to accept accepted practices and existing ways of doing things, whether in your personal life, business or society.

Few people want to question how things are done, for fear of being found wrong and looking silly.

"ATTRACT ATTENTION FROM THE CREW AT NIGHT?
PERISH THE THOUGHT! I'LL JUST KEEP ON TUTTING
AND SHAKING MY HEAD LIKE EVERYBODY ELSE TILL
THE LOUD WOMAN GETS THE CUE"

But progress is only achieved if you question orthodox thinking.

New concepts and ways of working come from challenging the status quo.

Being intellectually curious and open to new ideas helps to keep you excited, improving and relevant.

Clearly you need to gather data, do research and carry out sufficient analysis before making a decision to change something that has always been done a certain way.

Sometimes you'll stick with the existing approach but in many cases you'll decide to make a change.

You might be a lone voice advocating change initially, and you won't always be right, but at least you'll be moving forward.

You're fired!

Learning to let things go

My eldest daughter is quietly confident, with strong opinions - which she isn't afraid to express to me and my wife!

She will eventually leave home and become an independent young adult.

While we'll miss her when she does eventually leave home, we know that we have to learn to let her go.

But knowing you have to do something doesn't make it any easier.

A similar challenge arose with my business a few years ago.

Knowing when you need to leave a business which you created, nurtured, defended, financed and grew, can be just as emotionally painful and psychologically difficult than letting your children go - if not more so.

I started my financial advice business in 1998, and it was touch and go for the first five years.

Despite the significant initial challenges and many mistakes I made, the business became very successful.

As well as delivering a great service for clients it also rewarded me very well.

Beyond the obvious financial rewards the business also gave me intangible rewards – professional status, personal meaning, recognition, a sense of purpose and an outlet for my entrepreneurial vision and ideas.

The business almost became part of my identity, and my public persona was often defined in terms of the business.

However, a few years ago, as the business matured, the team grew and we institutionalised how the firm operated, I started to feel less and less excited about being part of it.

Looking back I can see that I blocked out these emotions and failed to acknowledge how I really felt.

I think part of it was the sense of obligation that I felt to the firm's clients, some of whom I had known for 25 years.

My mindset was very much one of being a custodian of the business.

The fact that I had removed myself from most of the day-to-day client work, and had assembled a fantastic team, didn't change the fact that I was the driving force and leader of the firm.

Clients did not have lots of daily contact with me, but they liked seeing or hearing my comments in the media.

They also knew that the firm had been built on my personal values and guiding principles.

Over time I started to envisage a different direction for my life which was not defined by my past, the expectation of other people, or money.

I have always been passionate about innovating, communicating, inspiring and creating.

I gradually realised that I could re-engineer my future by combining my passions with the skills and experience that I had acquired in my 25-year financial advice career.

This required me to accept that I could and should extract financial value from my stake to enable me to pursue my new life direction, rather than seeing myself as a custodian of the business.

Negotiating the exit from my business was not easy, and it took nearly a year.

But it is testament to the quality of what my colleagues and I had created that I eventually sold my stake to the other shareholders.

This minimised the impact on clients and staff, because the buyers knew the business well, and their purchase demonstrated to clients and staff their belief in and commitment to the firm.

After leaving the business, getting used to my new life has taken some adjusting and getting used to new routines and habits.

My professional speaking activity continues to grow and I am thoroughly enjoying engaging with and delivering value to my audiences.

I absolutely love giving a well-prepared talk which entertains, engages and delivers tangible value.

I've invested in a few start-up businesses, provided advice to some large businesses, and participated in various activities relating to young people and money.

I also have a regular wealth column in the Financial Times as well as writing for a range of other financial media.

I love the freedom, choice and variety which my new life now gives me.

"SIR, IT'S OKAY YOU JUST HAVE TO LET GO"
"BUT I FEEL LIKE IT WILL BE THE END OF ME!"

Every day is different and now I only do what I love and am good at.

Running a business can be exciting, rewarding, fun and enriching.

But I know only too well that sometimes it can also be a tough, stressful, thankless and lonely existence.

So what about you?

Are you living an outdated version of your life which is getting in the way of your happiness?

Are you being honest with yourself about what a good life really looks like?

Are you giving yourself excuses about why things can't be better?

If the life choices you have made are no longer serving you, then it's time to let them go.

You might find it necessary to fire yourself from your current role or job and start over anew.

It's all been rather lovely

A life well lived

"I have no regrets, because I've done everything I could to the best of my ability."

Robert Redford; actor, director and philanthropist

Bronnie Ware is an Australian nurse who worked for several years in palliative care, caring for people in the last three months of their lives.

Ware observed that people gain incredible clarity of vision at the end of their lives, and we can learn from this wisdom to improve our own lives, before it's too late.

"When questioned about any regrets they had or anything they would do differently," Ware says, "common themes surfaced again and again."

Ware wrote a book about the insights she gained from those at the end of their life, 'The Top Five Regrets of the Dying', to help others live a fuller life.

Here are the top five regrets of the dying, as witnessed by Ware:

1. I wish I'd had the courage to live a life true to myself, not the life others expected of me.

"This was the most common regret of all. When people realise that their life is almost over and look back clearly on it, it is easy to see how many dreams have gone unfulfilled. Most people had not honoured even a half of their dreams and had to die knowing that it was due to choices they had made, or not made. Health brings a freedom very few realise, until they no longer have it."

2. I wish I hadn't worked so hard.

"This came from every male patient that I nursed. They missed their children's youth and their partner's companionship. Women also spoke of this regret, but as most were from an older generation, many of the female patients had not been breadwinners. All of the men I nursed deeply regretted spending so much of their lives on the treadmill of a work existence."

3. I wish I'd had the courage to express my feelings.

"Many people suppressed their feelings in order to keep peace with others. As a result, they settled for a mediocre existence and never became who they were truly capable of becoming. Many developed illnesses relating to the bitterness and resentment they carried as a result."

4. I wish I had stayed in touch with my friends.

"Often they would not truly realise the full benefits of old friends until their dying weeks and it was not always possible to track them down. Many had become so caught up in their own lives that they had let golden friendships slip by over the years. There were many deep regrets about not giving friendships the time and effort that they deserved. Everyone misses their friends when they are dying."

5. I wish that I had let myself be happier.

"This is a surprisingly common one. Many did not realise until the end that happiness is a choice. They had stayed stuck in old patterns and habits. The so-called 'comfort' of familiarity overflowed into their emotions, as well as their physical lives. Fear of change had them pretending to others, and to themselves, that they were content, when deep within, they longed to laugh properly and have silliness in their life again."

Avoiding regrets should be a key priority for you while you can still do something about it.

John Le Mesurier, who played Sergeant Wilson in the iconic 1970s British comedy series 'Dad's Army', is reported to have said "It's all been rather lovely" before he passed away.

If you take heed of Bronnie Ware's insights, there is a very good chance that you'll be able to say the same thing when your time is up.

About the Author

Jason Butler is a Fellow of both the Personal Finance Society and Chartered Institute for Securities & Investment and had a 25-year career as a successful financial adviser.

Jason now focuses on speaking and writing about financial and personal wellbeing, as well as being an angel investor to various innovative financial technology start-up businesses.

Jason is the author of three personal finance books and is a columnist for the Financial Times, where as 'The Wealthman', he writes about personal finance related issues. He also provides expert comment on personal finance to the BBC and Sky and a range of other publications, media and websites.

Jason gives engaging and entertaining presentations, keynotes, and masterclasses on personal financial well-being and business innovation, which deliver tangible delegate takeaway value.

Jason lives in rural Suffolk with his wife, two daughters, two dogs and a horse.

 @jbthewealthman

Printed in Poland
by Amazon Fulfillment
Poland Sp. z o.o., Wrocław